Reaching

for

Air

# Reviews

I opened *Reaching for Air* and was stunned to attention. Gayle Lauradunn knows what she wants to say and how to say it. The reaching throughout. The not settling for what a person is given. The courage.

—Phyllis Hoge Thompson, author of seven poetry collections and an eighth *Hello, House* illustrated by Maxine Hong Kingston

ↂ

I love the portraits Gayle Lauradunn paints: the Texas Theater, Commerce Street, Mrs. Kretzmer's house.

—Art Goodtimes, first Poet Laureate of the Western Slope, Colorado and founder of Talking Gourds Poetry Festival

ↂ

Gayle Lauradunn continues to prove with this debut collection what those who know her poems have always suspected: that she communicates with messages to warm the heart with both an impressive generosity of spirit and an honesty of intention.

—Michael C. Ford, Pulitzer Prize nominated poet, playwright, editor, and Grammy nominated recording artist

*Reaching for Air* employs short, almost laconic sentences that create a kaleidoscopic portrait of an upbringing shaped by emotional and often physical abuse and the lifelong struggle of the recipient of that abuse to make sense of her experience and knit together a coherent sense of identity. Though the story told here is often bleak, the overall message is one of hope and redemption through the art of self-creation. A remarkably assured first collection.

—Richard Broderick, author of four poetry collections and recipient of the Minnesota Book Award

CR

# Reaching
## for
## Air

GAYLE LAURADUNN

*for*

*Quentin*

*and*

*Fiona*

Mercury HeartLink
www.heartlink.com

# Contents

## CLOSE AT THE CENTER

## WORLDS BEYOND

## INHERITANCE

## EPILOGUE

Some of these poems have appeared in the following journals and anthologies: *Puerto del Sol, Zone 3, Poetry From the Other Side, Cyclamens and Swords, Writers Forum 5, Tsunami, Adobe Walls, Trigger Warning: Poetry Saved My Life, The Rag, Writing Our Way Out of the Dark, Malpais Review.* And forthcoming, "Telling" in *Veils, Halos, and shackles: International Poetry on the Abuse and Oppression of Women.*

# Acknowledgments

With gratitude to those who have read and offered suggestions on some or all of these poems: Squaw Valley Writers' Conference, where these poems began; Group 18 (Doug Anderson, Ted Deppe, Jim Finnegan, Susan Finnegan, Linda Gregg. Margaret Lloyd, Robert Hill Long, Richard Michelson); Joan Larkin and Susan Tyler who both read the manuscript in great detail; Timothy Liu who first mentored these poems and suggested the original arrangement; Mary Ellen Kelly, Susan Barker, Julian Olf; Caroline LeBlanc, Jacqueline Loring, Kelly Yenser, Pamela Yenser; and with special appreciation to Louise Glück. for her incisive comments.

# PROLOGUE

# At the Zoo

At three
she rides an elephant.
The trunk wraps her
in an embrace
that soothes the tiny tears
and swoops her up
to the gypsy colored box.

She hears lions roar.
Beyond waving ears
she watches her parents
outside the fence.
They had pushed her forward
when the elephant master cast
his eye, and stand now,
arms around each other,
waiting.

In the dry-throat air
she clutches the colored edge,
crouches,
wanting outstretched arms.
The elephant lifts its feet
in rhythm with soft drumming,
sways its stately body
in a cradle song.

# THE
# TROTTER
# PLACE

# First Day

They move in August. The child
lugs sheets. Her father
and the men heave furniture
from the flatbed truck,
past the chicken
wire fence, into the house.

She sees in distance
that does not stop
the rising spiral of sand:
a snake walking on its tail.

The men hurry. Her mother
closes windows.
Between weathered boards
the child wiggles her fingers.
Sand coats
cracked linoleum.

At dusk sun lights
the rooms in long strips.
She brushes sand from the bed
into a bucket. Puts
on her nightgown
and turns back the sheet:
a scorpion crawls out.

# Suspension

On the porch of broken boards
the child arranges stones into patterns.

Inside her mother wanders
from room to room. She leaves

the house only to stand
on the porch. Rubs her hands.

With slow feet the child
enters. Dries the dishes,

flowers faded and chipped
as though ants had dined.

Watches the hands. Feels
the first sting on her cheek.

Feels the hard leather
on her legs. Long curls snatched

in the hand. She dances a high
jig against the belt.

Tears and pleas will break
the silence. She refuses.

# DEHORNING MOLLY

The child wanders
through the barnyard
clumped with chickens
pecking at each other
pecking their own shit
slinging it around.

The Jersey cow chews
quietly at the trough
her large brown sides
heaving slowly in and out
in the stark heat.
The child's hand
strokes in rhythm.
With her finger she
traces a white patch
over the nose.
Old Molly's tail switches
flicking flies
that swarm in the aroma
of cow, chicken, hog.

Into this animal world
the men come:
her father, her uncle,
the neighbor Mr. Renfrow.
They carry thick ropes
and a saw with jagged teeth.
A thick piece of lumber.

The child looks out to the field
sprouting white bolls.
A light breeze
stirs her hair.
Through the bellows
she hears
the rasp of the saw.

Later, her father said
she was too frisky,
butting into the barn,
tossing her head
as though those horns
meant something.

# WATER

The ice box drips,
drips, drips
in the kitchen.
The chunk of ice
already half melted
on the road from town.
Hauled by her father
in the rusty pickup
twice a week
with the wooden keg
of drinking water.

Three times a day
the air is disturbed
by the stir of spoons.
Steam from pots coats
the ceiling with sweat.
Her mother mixes
cornmeal with water and salt.
Fries it in bacon fat.

The windmill moans.
Blades circling the sky.

# CANDLING

In the kitchen at night
the child and her mother
hold eggs up to the single
bulb, the small brother
asleep in the next room.
Her parents came to this place
to raise turkeys.
Fat black ones
with red bumpy heads.
Carefully, she turns the egg,
almost as big as her hand,
looks through the thin
grainy shell for babies
that should not be there.
Sometimes she walks along
the fence following their
stiff-backed wanderings,
singing with them
their song.
As the eggs become fewer
she watches the turkeys
stumble about until they
fall and do not rise.
She watches the furrows
on her father's forehead deepen.
She looks at the five feathers

in the box by her bed.
Long, with narrow tips.
If she slants them
just right in the sun
she can see green and gold
dancing in the black silk.

# DISTANCE

She steps down
from the yellow bus
belching smoke,
runs across
the highway,
swings one thin leg
over the gate. Her
cotton panties snag
on the rough wood.

Centipedes
and blister bugs.
Tracks
of a diamondback.
She pauses
straddling the gate,
looks toward town.
The buildings
eight-mile distant.

Toward her house
on the rise
windmill blades
slice
through curdled air.

The sky, looming.

# JESUSA CHRISTA

There, in church, dressed in navy blue
With white ruffles, she hears, not the breath
Of angels, but the whispers and shuffles

That crowd the dark recesses of the transept.
Everywhere ladies in white gloves
And pursed lips. Men in dark suits

And muffled coughs. All sing Hosanna! Bless
The little children. Hosanna! Her legs
In white stockings to cover welts and bruises.

Hosanna! Blessed are the children. These
Precious gifts! Our heavenly father! Hosanna!

# CALICHE

The child leaves the house.
Leaves walls cracking
in her mother's hands.
Past the outhouse,
the chicken coop
to the softness of sheep.
In a mud hole the calf.
Chalk-white clay stiff
around its hooves. The one
her father missed. Flies
buzz over velvet sides,
the snow-soft face. Under
the mesquites sheep munch
grass nestled in patterns
of parched earth. Their *baa*
hangs in the air. The child
strokes the wet newborn.
It struggles to its first feet,
starts at the slipping snake.
Her hand hovers in the air.

# INHERITANCE

She leans against her father's
slat-backed chair as he quotes

*So I want you to swear, foul or fair,*
*You'll cremate my last remains.*

The kerosene stove swells and starts.
Roars again and pitches.

He herds them outside.
They stand shivering in moonlit snow

by the far fence while he
runs into the house. Wrestles

the stove like a black bear. Throws
open the door.

Flames soar
into the fair winter air.

## Summer Harvest

Tassels sear in the sun. Her father
walks the rows gathering ears. Tosses
them in a blue-flowered feed sack
that will become her dress.
In the wagon she climbs over
the iron clad wheel to touch
coarsened leaves. *Git back in there.*
Buzzards circle beyond and dive.
She waits. He climbs in, flaps
the reins with a click of his tongue.
The horse bolts. Pitches him
to the stony ground. She screams.
He stumbles upright. *Shut up.*
He stills the horse and again flaps
the reins. Seared tassels
crush beneath battered wheels.

# REFLECTIONS

In a blue flowered dress,
curving in at the waist,
flaring out at the hips,
she sits at the bare vanity
pulling her hair into a taut
chignon, parted at the middle,
tucked behind the ears,
black hair to cover the brown
rat. Fingers flutter over
the strands, the mirror
contorts, circles of sweat
under raised arms, legs cross
and cross again beneath crisp
cotton. In the mirror
the child watches the quick
straightening of the arm,
the sharp flash, the echoing crack.

# LOOKING
# FOR
# LIGHT

# THE GATE

She leans against the gate.
Places her arms carefully
on the rough wood. Rests her chin.
She clings, her small bottom
protruding, her pink dress blowing
in the hot breeze. The highway
runs in each direction
blending with the blue. She raises
one arm to read the indentations
in her reddened flesh. Arranges
the arm in a different position.
She strips a sliver. Jabs
its ragged tip into the board
in slow rhythm. In one direction
a dot grows into a car. Passes.
Soon becomes a dot again.
She climbs down from the gate
and tries as she does every day
to lift it. To watch it swing open.
Her thin arms tremble with
the weight. Drop to her sides. She
could climb over. Has many times.
Knows it is not the same.

# DRESSMAKER

Rigid, she stands
on the rickety chair.
Stares out the window
at the hotly milling turkeys.
Red wattles wobbling create
a breeze. Turn, the mother
mutters through a mouthful
of pins. The child's bare toes
inch over crinkled paint.
She adjusts her heels to match.
The mother smoothes the cloth.
Now the child's view
is the ice box. Light
filtering through the wall
brightens the daily accumulation
of dust on its top. The mother
pulls the cloth, snatches out
the pins. The child flinches.
Be still the mother mutters
and jabs the pins again.

## Gran'papa and the Sheep

Papa's short stout legs hurried us
to the lower pasture. My long skinny
ones stretched to keep up. "Papa, hurry,"
three year old Bobby shrieked
in his arms. We stumbled over scraggly
clumps of grass, through the mesquite
grove, the ground littered with speckled
beans. We could see the sheep gathered
in unruffled grazing. Papa slowed
to his usual amble and lowered
Bobby down. He rumpled one woolly
head, patted a fat side, put an arm
around the neck of another. With a soothing
voice he cleared a path. A moaning *baa*
summoned us. Papa knelt and tugged
at a tiny hoof. The ewe struggled.
"Hush. Hush." His arm disappeared,
popped out with a wet bundle squirming
in his hands. "Oh," Bobby said, hopping up
and down, "Papa made a baby."

# Whatever We Choose To Believe

The rock tower by the windmill
cool in summer. She forgets
until after she opens the door,
then catches her breath
against the acrid odor of urine.
The wee-wee pot for when
the outhouse is too far at night.
She pauses, chest swells,
eyes blink in the dimness.
She expels air slowly, takes
quick, shallow breaths as she
tiptoes across the concrete floor.
Shelves of empty canning jars.
A box of rusty tools. The trunk
filled with old clothes, evening
dresses discarded by the aunts.
Layering dress over dress
to make billowing hooped skirts,
the child enters the sunshine.
Shades her eyes with the folds
of a ripped fan, walks
with high carriage, skirts
raising dust, round
and round the tower. One hand
trailing over the rough stone.

# BOUNDARIES

She is everywhere outside
the house. Barn. Pigpen.
Chasing armadillos. Blond
pigtails bobbing. Farther
and farther away. Until she can
see in the distance the faint
outline of the Slater house.
Knows she has come as far as she
can. Walks to the barbed
wire fence. The dark line
where blue meets brown
never comes closer.
She jiggles the wire. Pricks
her finger. Sucks the saltiness.
She turns toward home.
Stops to pull stickers
from her feet. Tiny barbs
holding her to the ground.

# HOT AFTERNOON

The old mop handle
or the discarded broom,
either one will do.

The head's the important
thing. Granny
makes it from bright-

colored scraps
with big button eyes.
Bobby's Homer,

she's Eddy. With straw
hats hanging over their
ears and right hands drawn

they charge the hills
dispersing villainous ants,
destroying the quiet

of the fractured earth,
the ponderous air.
They stop to change horses

at the way station
but the chinaberry tree
yields nothing.

On they plunge across
country, sticks beating
a hard rhythm
between their legs.

# MOTHER/DAUGHTER

She watches her mother change
the tire on the old Chevrolet.
The rusty jack cranks and one side
of the back end rises slowly.
The jack slips onto the small finger
of her mother's left hand. A neat, clean cut
through the bone. The flesh. The blood.
The finger and its pink nail hang
for a moment by a white thread
before she grabs it with her right hand,
clamps it onto the stump, screams
Run, Run. The child frozen by the blood,
or the scream, or the car tilting.
Yells again. She runs. At first
stumbling then faster and faster
down the dirt road to the highway,
to the neighbors a mile away.

In the waiting room they watch her mother
walk out of the doctor's office, mouth
pinched. He sewed it on she said
and held up a fat white stalk seeping
red. The child wants to grab the gauze,
rip it off. Sling it out of sight
before the red seeps out of her, too.

# DREAMING OURSELVES

On Saturday afternoons
they shop in town. The week's
needs gathered in one trip.
The child is sent to the matinee
at the Texas Theater
near the courthouse square.
Inside the cool dark, she sits
on the end of a long row.
No one will block her get-a-way.
Hop-A-Long Cassidy. Lash LaRue.
The Lone Ranger and Tonto.
Mesquite. Sagebrush.
Dry-dust towns.
A world familiar,
yet new in its possibilities.
In her daydreams
she jumps on her horse,
throws a chap-clad leg over
the saddle in one smooth motion.
Rides. Until one Saturday
the marquee announces
Closed—Polio Epidemic.
The summer heat clings
holds the air to the ground.
She sits in the shade of the porch
breathing lightly,
riding far beyond the landscape.

# Redemption

On Sunday mornings she puts on the green
plaid dress from J.C. Penney's and clean
underpants. The family sits on a hard bench,
she next to her mother. Quiet. Still.
The minister speaks about fire and the right

hand of God. She holds the black hymnbook
in her lap, draws bluebonnets on it
with her finger. Gazes at the stained
glass window behind the minister's ample
white hair. Jesus on the cross, dripping

blood. Head hanging down, body limp.
She tugs at her underpants, too tight
for long sitting. The minister's voice
thunders the Word of God "And the Word
was made flesh." She has watched blood

drip from the pig strung up in the barn,
head crooked on its broad neck. Bacon
and pork chops, salt pork to season beans.
Her mother drips blood from between her
legs, has told her she will, also.

The minister passes out the wafers
of flesh, the red juice. She squeezes her
thighs together. Accepts a wafer. Feels
the hand of God descending. Carefully she
crushes the wafer between her fingers.

# Sunday Drive

The air tightens inside the black car.
In the back seat the child and her brother
press against opposite corners. The father
drives. Behind him she watches his neck,
the back of his head. She knows when his
jaw flexes. The mother stares straight
ahead. The brother mouths words of Burma
Shave signs. The child clenches her fists
in her lap, looks out the window
as a field of bluebonnets flashes by. She
speaks of bright blue-purple. It's just
flowers the father yells. The mother jerks
her head around. Eyes glaring.

# DOLL

Each year for Christmas
They give her a doll
A baby doll
A lady doll
A fluffy doll

When she asks
About the book
They say
She is ungrateful
When she asks
About the blocks
They say
She is a girl

Each year the day
After Christmas
She places the doll
On the shelf
And walks out
To see the light
Dance through leaves

Walks to find the sheep
In huddles

Treads her way
To sit on rock piles

Sheltering
Sleeping snakes
In the midday sun

# CLOSE
## AT
## THE CENTER

# Chicken Every Sunday

To Grandmother and Granddaddy's
every Sunday for two years after
Oliver    the firstborn
was killed in the car crash
He looked down to light a cigarette
and smashed into the oncoming
watermelon truck
The mixture of pink and red painted
the narrow gray highway
for weeks    there was a drought that year
The green Plymouth was half its
newborn length when they hauled
it back to town    it sat on Commerce St.
near the G & R Market    for months
it seemed    I never did know
what happened to it

The forty-five minute drives
from Brady to San Saba
began after church    to comfort
the old folks    Mama was oldest now
and had that responsibility
Newell and now Oliver
dead    the two boys    and now
a girl for oldest
Every Sunday as we climbed
out of the black Chevrolet
my stomach churning with the dust

of crooked roads
Grandmother would holler
to Granddad    *Op, fetch*
*me a hen so's I kin*
*fix dinner.*

Op, fingers crooked from a half-century
of cranking tractors and old cars,
reached out among the yard full
of white leghorns    stifled
one set of cackles with a firm
grip to the neck
his outstretched arm wound
wide and fast like a ball pitcher
aiming for a strike call
After three rounds his arm
snapped back    leaving in his hand
two shiny staring eyes    a yellow
beak and a red comb
The white ball of feathers flew
high    I ran to peer out from
behind the smokehouse    watch
dumbly while the headless
body flopped and ran    flopped
and ran    the bony throat
a fluid spurting siren

## Summer Rain

In the house with no plumbing
her grandmother hands out
bars of lye soap to the family.
Each one strips to underwear
runs outside to find
a place behind barn, smokehouse,
chicken coop. The child
splashes through quick-formed
puddles to the pigpen.
Pigs roll and squirm
as their mud hole grows.
She passes the soap
slowly over arms, stomach,
down the inside of her thighs
as she twirls round and round
savoring. Toes pressed
into mud, she
lifts her face to the sky.
Opens her mouth to sweetness.

# RED-GOLD IN SUNLIGHT

She drives north with Granddaddy
to Comanche County. His gnarled hands
easy on the steering wheel. To buy
peaches for pies and canning. They tramp
orchard after orchard tasting this one
and that. Thick grass wet. Socks and shoes
soaked. The child breathes deep of red-gold
fragrance held in sunlight. The men
bargain. Argue the value of varieties.
Granddaddy's hands gesture the air. Her
mouth and lips sting from the thick
fuzz. Her stomach roils. He offers
yet another peach. She shakes her head.
He pushes the golden fruit into her mouth,
the softness hard against her teeth.

# The Lesson

On the floor next
to the Singer the child
counts her fingers,
inhales the oiliness.

Her mother corrects,
her right foot
working the treadle.
Toes up and down.
The machine starts.
Whirrs. Stops.

The child counts
slowly beyond
her fingers to one
hundred. Numbers
float into barren
heat. With each
mistake the needle
staccato increases.
Jabs in and out.

A neat line of tiny holes
extending beyond
the fingers.

# TELLING

Sometimes I think I made it up. Try to convince myself that
      he didn't hurt me
that mother didn't turn on me, didn't yell to a five-year-
      old "how could you let him do that?"
or the old man didn't exist, or the old man didn't do it.
I remember my lack of fear, the pleasure, telling
      mother.
He could have been 40 or 70. A deaf mute who must have
      wanted to experience as much of life as possible.
      Being left out of sound.
But, no, he was just a dirty old man.
I only remembered this experience again after many years
      and now it won't leave me.
That old man's face haunts me. I see it even with my eyes
      closed. I couldn't have made it up.
He was tall and slender, almost thin, and wore khaki work
      shirt and pants with a brown belt, wide leather
with a gold buckle. The shirt had seven buttons down
      the front, tan buttons.
His hands were large, square with thick hair on the fingers.
      His fingers warm and gentle inside my panties.
His face had deep lines, the flesh leathery. His
      thin hair black.
He hurt me. He wasn't gentle. But, no, mother stops him
she stops him just as he reaches under my dress. No, she
      stops him just as he pulls down my panties.
She grabs his arm, jerks it away. Screams at him. He runs
      away. He is back
with his hand between my legs, his fingers digging.

His fingers inside me and I am laughing.
I am daddy's Baby Doll. I am crying. I am pushing against
        him. I am running.
Every man I meet has a lined face. Every man I bed has hairy
          fingers.
I laugh, cry, with every man. Mother, where are you? No.
          This scene is all wrong. It is a hot July afternoon.
The old man sits with my baby brother asleep in his lap. I
        am five.
No one else is in the house. The doors and windows open.
          Light is everywhere in my grandparents'
house. He is granddaddy's cousin. He wanders and works
          where he can in his boots,
high topped, laced around the ankles. He is quiet. He grins.
          A Halloween mask. Some teeth
stained with tobacco. Outside, the windmill creaks.
          No. It wasn't a dress.
It was a pinafore with lacy ruffles on the shoulders. A
          blue pinafore with white eyelet trim
and white buttons. I was five. He motioned me to him
          pointed to the baby asleep.
He pulled up my dress, put his hand in my panties.
          No. We were outside,
down the hill in the woods behind the house. I followed
          him out into the wavering heat.
I wanted to know his silence. The baby wasn't there. My
          dress was yellow.
It was my panties that were blue. His belt was drawn tight
          around his waist, his pants gathered.
It was there in the dry grass that he did it. Yes, I'm
        sure.
I'm sure. I was wearing a blue and yellow check sunsuit
          and my panties were white. White.

# HEAT

We cool our bodies
in mud-red rivers
silt-gritty and thick,

weeds trailing. Toes dance
in ooze pebble nicked.
Above, cottonwoods

embrace stilted air.
We splash each other
with glee, seeking ease,

happy in the gamble
we take. I float on
my back, hair fanned out

like tendrils of weeds.
    Flash of cottonmouth.
        The sudden tangle.

# GIFT

Three times a year.
Christmas.
Easter.
Birthday.
Granny sends Little
Golden Books.
Fifteen cents each.
The child knows it is a lot.

She thumbs the pages
until their edges rag.
Then the fat treasury
of verses for children
arrives. She strokes
the words until they
imprint her fingers.

One day the book is
gone. She finds it later
shredded in the trash bin.

Lays her hands
on the tatters.
Ruffles the edges.

# WARM WIND RISING

Winged pigweed Granny says.
Russian thistle Mother says.

The child knows it is neither.
She knows it is dead. Dry

and brittle. Like the air.
She watches for it when she

walks the land. Picks her way
between prickly grasses.

She sits on her haunches
at the giant ant hill,

watches. Fat and shiny.
When they all disappear down

the hole she stands
to meet the warm wind rising.

Sees the grass come alive,
roll into balls, and rush

toward her. One strikes

her leg.  Blood trickles down

a bare ankle. She begins to run
and run. The wind carrying her

tumbling over the land.

# CONSECRATION

The child makes her way to the outhouse.
Bare feet blench at pebbles.
Red ants. Large as her thumbnail.
Inside she sits on the oval edge.
The wood cool in its smoothness. Leans
her chest toward her knees. Feet
dangle. She turns her head,
sees through cracks of gray boards
thin shimmer of air. After
the cramping passes she eases
white panties over scabbed knees.
Scoops from the 50-pound bag pressed
into the corner. Facing the dark hole,
she sprinkles the powdery lime
in a circle that closes at the center.

# BREAKING AWAY

The child straddles
the bay, her blue dress
rises up her thighs,
nudges sharply
with bare heels.
Patsy prances
through the gate,
tosses her head
as though to sniff
the wider air.
The child wraps
her hands
in the long black mane
and tugs.
Heels dig deeper
and Patsy
shifts to a trot.
The child looks back
to see the house
shrink.
No longer hears
her mother's
mother's voice
marking the smallness
of her body,
the flex
of her fingers.
Muscles beneath

the red-brown coat
ripple across her thighs.
She tightens them,
leans her cheek
against the warmth.
Breathes the body smell.
They weave through mesquite
and prickly pear.
As they near the rise
Patsy pauses at the top
then lengthens her stride
and gallops
into the distance,
the child resting
in the heat of flesh and wind.

# WORLDS
# BEYOND

# Moving

She arrives home
from school to boxes

stacked on the parquet floor.
Walks to her room.

The boxes there
she fills with paper dolls

she has drawn,
cut out, colored in fine

dresses.
With books

she takes
from town to town.

In every room
boxes rise

and deplete the air.
Their sides enclose

her. She breathes
their musty glue.

The dark she walks into.

## Catlettsburg: Above the Garage

Her narrow bed presses against the foot
of the larger bed spread with white
chenille. Her playground the wood floor
from wall to wall. Beans cooking
and salt pork. Steam clots the air.
Her mother stands in the kitchen
doorway and looks at the child who
stands in the bedroom looking at her.
Starched dresses clutter the closet
around the heavy navy blue coat
buttoned to the neck. By climbing
onto the sofa she can see out the window.
Trees in the wind, breathing.

# A MOUNTAIN INSIDE

At the nursery school door
she clutches her blanket.
Sniffs her sleep smell.
Light through high windows cuts
bar patterns on the walls.
A teacher pulls her by the hand
to a group around blocks.
Pushes her shoulders to the floor.
Numbers and letters indent
her fingers. She stacks faded
squares. A mountain she sees inside.
Stream. Trees. Birds.
The teacher's hand knocks the blocks
over. Shows her how
to arrange them. The concrete
floor seeps cold through her dress,
her panties. She knows
the roundness of her bottom. She
is quiet. At lunch the macaroni
warms her throat. She asks
for more. A finger points
to the uneaten collards. Swirling
in grease. Coloring the room.

# Two Tales of Black

Her father leaves for work in the dark,
returns in the dark. In Ashland,
Kentucky they have a kitchen and bedroom.
The day stretches back and forth
between the rooms. To keep the child quiet
her mother reads fairy tales and rhymes.
She always asks for the gypsies.

The
     raggle-
          taggle-
               gypsies-
                    O.

The fine lady with a fine house
and servants, a fine husband and carriage
who runs away with the black-haired gypsies.

     Raggle-
          taggle-
               gypsies-
                    O.

If she is good, she can play
under the oak for half an hour
while her mother stands on the veranda
knuckles white on the coffee cup.

Taggle-
       gypsies-
            O.

Until the day the minister comes.
In his black suit. His insistent voice
and before she knows it she is walking
behind him every morning to Vacation
Bible School where she does not speak.
The children line up with backs pressed
against the brick wall to receive
the graham cracker and half cup of milk.
She follows the black suit back to the rooms.

      Gypsies-
        O.

# Reaching for Air

Sometimes when her parents play cards
she stays overnight with Mrs. Timmons,
takes with her a can of Campbell's soup.
Mrs. Timmons sits at the table,
moon face unsmiling, heavy body poised,
until the child finishes the whole can,
lukewarm and thick. When the two
daughters come home from work
they hang puff-sleeve dresses in the closet,
smooth out wrinkles for tomorrow.
They sleep in their slips, the child
between them in flannel pajamas,
their backs to each other and to the child
who wakes. She holds her breath
until they settle the covers and waits
for the familiar heat to bring sweat,
waits to push the covers down.
The glow from the street light
illuminates the white slips and the deeper
white of the bra and panties beneath.
She looks for dampness on their backs
which do not move all night. Pushing
with her feet she inches upward
until the headboard presses her hair.
She releases the two top buttons,
spreads the damp cloth.

# Eagle Mountain Lake

## I

That morning, among empty
and full boxes, her mother
found a razor blade.
Made a cut across the tips
of her white high-top shoes.
To let her toes grow straight.
The other children titter
and point. Run away from her.
The laughter again. The deep
drag of the shiny razor.
The recoil of her toes. Turning
away from the taunts she tucks
woolly bear under her arm.
Trudges to the wooden beach chair
where she sits to watch water
hug the sand. The rowboat,
its long rope tied to the chair,
nods up and down. She wiggles
her toes in the blue socks.
Murmurs to bear: sky,
water, boat. Rising,
she wanders down the slope.
Waits as the water crawls
to her. Feels the cool
lick through blue cloth.

They move from the water-edged
cabin to the house up the hill.

Empty rooms with large windows
latticing the lake.

Shoes pat-pat on the bare floor
as she walks from room to room

tracing the wallpaper with one
wet finger. Somewhere her
mother unpacks boxes.

The dull rustle of paper
mars the silence the rooms
wrap around her.

She blows on a window pane,
draws a stick figure.

Beyond, children build
sand castles, the yellow globe

slips down the sky
sinks into water.

She sucks in her breath

as though to erase the figure.
Dries her finger on her skirt.

Over the soft lapping
of water, lights
flicker like bouncing balls.

# Pickling

Her father turns the soil in the small
garden. Melons and tomatoes.
He takes the black-spined
cucumbers into the kitchen. The child
heaps them on the counter:
fat green worms that do not move.
Her father cleans and salts them
puts them in a large pot. Steam
bubbles through the house. It is
to make the cukes last a long time.

Three times a day her mother
eats calcium powder by the tablespoon
from a dark jar. Each time
she gags. It is to make the baby
strong she says. Did you make
me strong the child asks,
Hush, this baby will be a boy.
Help me now to clean the house.
The child walks through doorways.
Every room smells of vinegar and milk.

# ANOTHER HOUSE

Her father soaks the mattress
with kerosene to kill the bugs,
layers newspapers, spreads the sheets.
Her mother rocks the baby close.
The child leans against the chair
watches shadows crawl across
the contours of new shapes.
A bus, a train, a taxi

brought them to this tiny house.
Three rooms in a line from
the street to the outhouse
they share with the hobo shelter
next door. For fear she will
catch something her mother gives
her an old soup pot to pee in.
From across the street Lizann,

seven years to the child's five,
brings her treasure box:
broken rhinestone pin,
one long purple earring,
half-used tube of lipstick.
The child cannot imagine
these as treasures. Instead
she stands at the window
watches the men come and go
at Lizann's mother's house,

a large blank building
with small windows like
the upstairs rooms in cowboy
movies. From the other window
she watches hobos leave
in early morning, watches
new ones arrive at dusk.
Sometimes one walks to the
outhouse. They wear suspenders
and patched coats. They don't
shave. They travel wherever
they want to. She begs
to use the outhouse. Her mother
relents and takes her. She tries
to reach from footprint
to footprint, measuring the stride
she will need to walk out
of El Dorado, Arkansas.

# Fairy Tales

Every afternoon when her mother
takes the baby outside she pushes
a brown chair to the white refrigerator
and stands on it to reach the knob
on the box radio. "Just Plain Bill"
is announced. Voices people
the house. The jingle as someone
enters Bill's barber shop and settles
for a gossip. Molly cries when Rick
leaves but carries on. Dan was in
a fight. Badly hurt. It is what comes
at the end that draws her every day:
the gentle touch she can almost see.

## ALL THAT IS LIGHT

They live in half of Mrs. Kretzmer's house,
three rooms in a row. While her mother cooks
ham hocks and mustard greens, she kneels
on a chair by the window, watches the goats,
white and bleating, their old men's beards
dancing as they chew. Watches the goats
clatter among broken-down sheds, piles
of tossed boards and tin cans. The dark
interiors, the bright relief of goats. Mrs.
Kretzmer knocks on the kitchen door, looks
at the mother, takes the child by the hand
down the steps into the yard. Releasing her,
she beckons her to follow, and enters
a shed. The child stays by the gate. One goat
watches. Finally, she emerges with a bucket,
squats by the goat, beckons sharply with knotted
fingers she then bends around full teats.
A step at a time the child nears until the wiry
softness is beneath her hand. The gentle
breathing. She follows the sloshing bucket
to the screened porch. A quiet command seats
her at a table. Mrs. Kretzmer pours two tall
glasses of milk and sips. Slowly the child's
tongue tips the frothy surface. Later,
when she tells how quickly she drank all the milk,
about the coolness, the whiteness, her father's

voice thunders against the smallness
of goats, the whimper of their bleats, their
scraggly beards. The child looks out
out the window. All is dark.

# Two Worlds

Her father goes deep
into the river
bound in the heavy suit.
His eyes look out
the window of the helmet
locked on his head.
The child watches
from the bank. Sees
long hoses send him
to rushing water.
On the bottom
he swims with fish
and builds a bridge.
The skirt of her mother's
brown and white
checkered dress stirs
in the wind.
The child grabs the hem
in a fist. The sun glances
from tin hats of men
slogging through mud.
A bulldozer crashes
into a hillside
leaves a pile of boulders.
Backs up, crashes again.
The steam shovel scoops,
turns its awkward head,

dumps. Men shout.
The water surges white
as a windlass
winds up the hoses.
Armored suit kicks
and flails. Dark water
reaches for feet.
She twists the cloth tighter.
Hides her face
in its folds.
Someone steps up,
twists the helmet and lifts it
from her father's head.
She can hear his laughter
as the men gather round.
Joking.
The laughter echoes
through the dark.

# GARDEN

The child and her friend
plan a garden
in the empty lot
between their houses.
Weeds up to their waists.
They pull.
Dig with hand spades
until a plot appears.
They decide on their crop:
radishes, scallions,
marigolds, zinnias.
Plant seeds in rows of two.
They carry pots of water.
The wet soil black next
to the dry white-brown.
Under the live oak nearby
they munch peppery radish.
Strip scallions
and weave necklaces
of green and white.
Marigolds behind their ears,
in their waistbands.
Zinnias in tall canning jars
on kitchen tables.
Everything grows
in the passing summer:
garden, weeds, girls.
Later, after hot winds

brush the land
she returns to the garden.
Weed-choked and dry.
One cracked radish coloring.

# Imperfect Clarity

At the doorway the child drops
down on all fours. The waxed
boards hard. As she crawls
slowly toward the pallet

her hem catches under her knees.
She tugs at it with one hand.
In the twilight room her mother
weeps. She is a shape

curved on layers of quilts.
The child's words whisper
out the window. She
curves onto the pallet.

Her breath follows
the rhythm of weeping.
Soon stars light the sky.
She holds out a finger

to touch the brightness
she cannot reach. Turning
she traces a luminous
stain on her mother's cheek.

# INHERITANCE

# The Visit

I take my small son, raised
on dark New England woods
to my genesis under west Texas

sky. He shrinks in this alien landscape
while I can breathe again.
The car rumbles over a cattle guard

and he asks, as I once did,
where, then, are the cows?
I tell him they gave up long ago.

His blue eyes widen as though
measuring my idea of cows. He
does not want to enter the house

with the red roof half caved in.
I take his hand and lead him where
I walked. I want him to understand

my need for air. As we pass
through bare rooms he tightens
his grip. Outside he tries to climb

the windmill. Rotting wood sticks
to his hands. He settles instead
for the low branches of the old mesquite.

On the sheep-graze we find my refuge,

the oak clump of childhood solitude.
I tell him to keep walking

if we see a rattler. It is harmless
if uncoiled. I forget he has not known
this since he could walk. His tears

surprise me. I point to shapes
in the clouds, in the sky
that surrounds him. On the ground

he draws in the dirt with his finger,
refuses to look up. His eye unused
to travelling so far.

## LAURA AND ROBERT

Granny and Papa and eight children
follow the cotton blooms
from Texas to Arizona and back.
Sometimes they stop for Papa

to set up barbering and Granny
to plant a garden, stretching twine
for purple morning glories.
The kids walk to school,

three or four miles, barefoot
in the dust. Until Granny begins
to fidget and sigh and eye
the distance. Without a word

Papa packs his shears and combs
and the next day the teacher
wonders where those kids
are. Years after Papa died

Granny said, "The happy times?
When my kids' bellies were full."
She looks out the window at the horizon
she has travelled toward for ninety years.

# Going Home

Oldest of Laura's eight,
Dad's feet itched for new ground.
Mother went without a word
railed her fury at me.

Settled in a town for a few weeks,
he'd return from work excited
about a new place he'd heard of.
Mother's mouth became a thin line.

A slender man, cigarette in hand,
walking quickly, hammering, planting,
talking with any stranger as to a
brother or sister, gesturing.

Without travel, an edge crept
into his voice. I backed away
from its cut, from Mother's hand.

His eyes search the distance,
neck quivering in his still body.

# Presence

Little Grandmother is scarcely taller
than the child who follows her
from the bed, piled with softness,
to the bathroom of medicine bottles,
and back again, many times a day,
the careful step, the shrunken chest.
She hears the silence as though
this great-grandmother is tired
of speaking to children. Ten children
fathered by the tall, thin man
in the photograph above the bed.
She sleeps upright against a mound
of pillows. To breathe. The child
wants to touch the sparse white hair
twisted into a knot at the top
of her head. Touch the skin
so wrinkled. Jiggle into motion
with her finger the tight lips. To hear
them say Yes, I know you're here.

# GRANDFATHER

Grandfather sits in the nursing home, his wheelchair
      strapped down so he won't rock himself to the floor
   again and hit his head gash it open, open, he

wants to see the blood. He rips the pajamas covering
      the stumps to look for his legs. At eighty-eight he
   threw his last calf for branding, his fingers losing

their quickness, their quickness with the rope and
      the calf kicked him shattering his hip. He planted
   corn and alfalfa, raised five children, two

children to their death. He slaughtered cows, pigs,
      wrung, wrung necks of chickens. He asks now
   he asks whose girl are you I'm Annie B's

Grandpa Annie B's. And he asks how old am I
      how old. Ninety-seven Grandpa ninety-seven.
   Too old he says too old whose girl are you

Annie B's Grandpa Annie B's. Too old he says too
      old and rocks, rocks hard the chair tied to the floor.

*Aunt Sal*
   *1778-1873, a freed nigra*

As you can see my stone
is smallest and most worn.
Yes, I was first at Harmony
Ridge to be put underground.
Lucky they didn't leave me
behind in Carolina, old and useless
as I was. Most of the way I
laid on a mattress in the back
of the Conestoga. Times
we thought I wouldn't make it.
I near raised those three Oliver
boys and them and their wives
and passel of children took kindly
to me. I was mighty glad when
we come to this fertile ridge
with the river running nearby.
Only scorpions in the bedrolls
and rattlers ready to strike
disturbed us. The boys set up
tents then built the one-room
for church. More children come,
forty-six in all. Then another room
for schoolhouse. Live oaks
and mesquites gave shade for me
to sit under. I could shell
peas to help a bit. But I give
out afore the houses was built.
So the cemetery was started
for me. Yes, I was first
but I'm the only one.

# First Funeral

Men roll cigarettes beneath straw
Stetsons. Women tie on aprons
and bustle food to long tables.
To the side of one table, a long dark
box. Grasping its edge the child
pulls up on tiptoes. Great-Grandmother
asleep on a small pink pillow,
hands folded. Lips tightly closed.
The child reaches out to touch
a wrinkled cheek. Someone jerks
her hand away. She waits.
Reaches out again for the feel of death.
Prods it to hear it speak.

## Punch Lines

Great-Uncle Buddy keeps us all entertained
with his stories. Like the one about Joey down
on the Brazos. The room bright with sun
and fresh air blowing the lacy curtains, we laugh
so hard tears roll down our cheeks. Tiny blue
flowers paper the walls. Everyone relaxes
as the latest jokes toss about. Uncle Buddy
leads off and goes one better every time. My
cousins and I play in the corner, joining in
as though we get the punch lines. The old
comfortable chairs. A few more to surround
the great white bed where he lies in fetal position.
Thrown from a mule at seventeen he has lain
for forty years on one side then the other. A small
fat pillow between his bony knees. His spidery
fingers web the air. The skin stretches
over his parchment face as he grins
with the humor he's invented to keep us there.

# HERITAGE

In the photograph my son and I stand
in Great-Great-Granddad's corn crib
built of poles glossy from years
of corn-husk polishing, ears fresh picked
to age for cattle feed, side by side
we face the camera, my arm across
his shoulder, my hand rests lightly there.

We stare beyond, as though to see the people
in sun-faded overalls walk the whispery
rows in west Texas heat, and I like to think,
in his child way, he understands what we do,
that he hears them call to each other
down the rows, that he brings their voices
with him into his music, those inward
songs children make of their world.

# EPILOGUE

BIRTH RITE


she didn't admit
i was there tunneling
inside her
until too late
and he came home from work
caught her
with a tin spoon
eating
dirt between the honeysuckle
and the weathered fence

perhaps being bred on worms
is ok   it gives me
my love of nature
my desire to be in the woods
in the mountains
near the ocean

perhaps it's why i like
to squat on impulse
near loose soil
scoop it up
run it through
my fingers
i need to examine
each particle
look for the particular
relationship

and i look for worm eggs
or nests of baby worms waiting
to be fed
i expect to see worms
copulating
grinning at me through

air spaces then on all fours
i begin to dig
furiously
for the spoon has a head start
and i must catch its light
before dark

but as usual i've started
on reflex
and have only my fingers
for tools
they are thin and bony
and the nails break easily
as they dig
each finger grows
longer   carves
a path

i hunch closer to the ground
my fingers feel the dirt's
shape
identify fragments
and wiggle deeper
soon they disappear
i flatten my stomach

to the ground
follow their tunnels

they are at home in the dark
slowly my arms sink
into the dirt
a soft slither startles me
worms creep up and
over my back
at first a few but finally
hundreds
i nod good day
and go on digging

the ridges of my knuckles
flex
each finger drops off
at the joint and
inches away
worms basking
on my back slough off
and dig beside me
the tunnels stretch
into a glow
ahead i see a spoon

Gayle Lauradunn reinvents herself about every five to seven years. Along the way she was co-organizer of the first National Women's Poetry Festival, a 6-day event held at the University of Massachusetts, Amherst in 1974. While there she earned an Ed.D. For her dissertation she used 20th Century American poetry to create a curriculum to teach high school students about race, class, and gender. She learned about the crossover of race and class while living in the poor Black ghetto in Nashville, Tennessee. For five years she participated in the editorial collective that published *Chomo-Uri: A Women's Literary and Arts Journal*.

After earning a B.A. in English Literature at the University of California, Berkeley, she became a feature writer for a weekly newspaper, and over the next 20 years worked as a free-lance journalist. Her anti-Vietnam War activism led her to become Executive Director of the Veterans Education Project, a group of Vietnam, Korean, and Desert Storm veterans who spoke to high school students about the realities of war and military service.

As a single parent, she travelled extensively with her son throughout the United States, camping, backpacking, white water rafting, exploring museums and historical sites. An avid traveller, she has been to all 50 states and more than 20 countries, Bhutan and Antarctica being her favorites to date.

Her poems have been published in numerous journals, anthologies, and online. This is her first book. She is writing a book-length narrative poem about a historical figure. In 1998 she moved to New Mexico where she follows the changing light and shadows as the sun moves across the Sandia Mountains.